ABT

D0803452

3/08

EXTREME LIFE

SURVIVING DEATH VALLEY

DESERT ADAPTATION

BY PAMELA DELL

Consultant:
Lynn F. Fenstermaker
Associate Research Professor
Desert Research Institute
Las Vegas, Nevada

Capstone
press

Mankato, Minnesota

Fact Finders are published by Capstone Press,
151 Good Counsel Drive, P.O. Box 669, Mankato, Minnesota 56002.
www.capstonepress.com

Library of Congress Cataloging-in-Publication Data
Dell, Pamela.
    Surviving Death Valley : desert adaptation/ by Pamela Dell.
    p. cm. — (Fact finders. Extreme life)
    Summary: "Describes adaptations that occur in the desert environment, including general
adaptations and examples" — Provided by publisher.
    Includes bibliographical references and index.
    ISBN-13: 978-1-4296-1266-1 (hardcover)
    ISBN-10: 1-4296-1266-5 (hardcover)
    1. Desert biology — Death Valley (Calif. and Nev.) — Juvenile literature. 2. Desert ecology —
Death Valley (Calif. and Nev.) — Juvenile literature. 3. Adaptation (Physiology) — Death Valley
(Calif. and Nev.) — Juvenile literature. I. Title. II. Series.
QH88.D44 2008
578.75409794'87 — dc22
                                                         2007023628

Editorial Credits

Jennifer Besel, editor; Alison Thiele, designer; Linda Clavel, photo researcher

Photo Credits

Bruce Coleman Inc./Edward L. Snow, 26 (gecko); Bruce Coleman Inc./Hal Beral-V&W, 25; Desert
Research Institute, 28 (left); Dreamstime/Bigmax, 22; Dreamstime/Pomortzeff, 18; Getty Images
Inc./Minden Pictures/Michael & Patricia Fogden, 14; Getty Images Inc./Minden/Tom Vezo,
27; Getty Images Inc./Stone/Tim Flach, 13 (bottom); iStockphoto/Angela Cable, 8–9; Minden
Pictures/AUSCAPE /D. Parer & E. Parer-Cook, 23; Minden Pictures/Michael & Patricia Fogden,
20–21; Minden Pictures/npl/Barry Mansell, 19; Minden Pictures/npl/Neil Bromhall, 24; Minden
Pictures/Tom Vezo, 15; Nature Picture Library/Tom Vezo, 17; Peter Arnold/Cal Vornberger, 16;
Peter Arnold/John Cancalosi, 10, 13 (top); Photo Researchers, Inc/Steve & Dave Maslowski, 4–5;
Shutterstock/Andy Heyward, 26 (notebook); Shutterstock/Brad Thompson, 11; Shutterstock/
Dimitriadi Kharlampiy, 26 (binoculars); Shutterstock/Helder Joaquim Soares de Almeida, 6;
Shutterstock/PSHAW-PHOTO, 7; Shutterstock/Robyn Mackenzie, 26 (hat); Shutterstock/Rusty
Dodson, cover; Shutterstock/Winthrop Brookhouse, 28–29 (right)

1 2 3 4 5 6 13 12 11 10 09 08

TABLE OF CONTENTS

CHAPTER 1

DESERT EQUALS DRY

You're lost in the desert. The temperature is well above 100 degrees Fahrenheit (38 degrees Celsius). The only plants you see are cactuses. But their spines are so sharp you can't eat them. And water. There's no water anywhere. Will you survive?

No, you probably wouldn't survive. But if you think that nothing could survive in the desert, you're wrong. Some plants and animals have **adapted** to a life with high temperatures and almost no water.

Need a sneak peek? Cactuses store gallons of water in their stems. Roadrunners get water by eating the guts of lizards and snakes. Some animals stay cool by sleeping when the sun is out. Others stay cool by peeing on themselves.

adapt: to change in order to survive

Deserts cover about one-third of the land on our planet. And plants and animals have adapted to life in almost every corner of this dry land. Let's take a closer look at some of the deserts that creatures call home.

Thirsty? Try a roadrunner's lizard smoothie.

DESERT AREAS

DESERT

CRAZY!

Some spots in the Atacama Desert in Chile have gone 400 years without rain.

Deserts Near and Far

Deserts are found on all seven continents. Some are hot, while others are cold. But they are all super dry. In fact, deserts never get more than 10 inches (25 centimeters) of rain all year.

One of the largest deserts in the world is the Sahara. Located in northern Africa, the Sahara is bigger than the entire continental United States. But this desert isn't just big. It's hot too. Average summer temperatures reach 122 degrees Fahrenheit (50 degrees Celsius).

It might look pretty, but without water and shade it would be Death Valley for you too.

Death Valley is part of the Mojave Desert in the western United States. This place never gets more than 4.5 inches (11 centimeters) of rain. And it's hot. In the mid-1800s, many miners died trying to cross this desert. That's how Death Valley got its name.

The miners died because people are not adapted to life without water. But some animals and plants are. Desert creatures have some fascinating tricks that keep them alive in the driest places on earth.

CHAPTER 2

AMAZING ADAPTATION

Adaptations don't happen overnight. You see, changes that help an animal survive are passed down from parent to child in their DNA. If a particular body part or behavior isn't helping, then it slowly disappears from the species over time.

Animals and plants adapt in two main ways. Sometimes changes affect the way they look. Physical adaptations might change an animal's coloring or the shape of its mouth. It might even mean developing a really big bladder that can hold a lot of pee. For plants, it might mean developing stems that can expand to hold lots of water when it finally rains.

Pronghorn antelope match their dusty yellow surroundings. This physical adaptation helps them hide from predators.

DNA: material in cells that gives animals their individual characteristics

species: a type of insect, animal, or plant

cactus wren

Other adaptations affect how an animal or plant behaves. Parents teach their young some behavioral adaptations. Cactus wrens teach their young how and where to nest. Plant behaviors are also about survival. When it rains, seeds on the desert floor spring to life. When they bloom, they spread new seeds that will bloom with the next rain.

INTERVIEW WITH A CAMEL

INTERVIEWER: I'm here in the Sahara Desert. I've just caught up with a camel. Excuse me while I take a drink of water.

CAMEL: Too bad you can't drink water like me. I can gulp 30 gallons (that's 114 liters) of water in 15 minutes. I'm a record holder.

INTERVIEWER: Wow! That must be how you survive in the desert.

CAMEL: That's part of it. Camels have lived in the desert a long time, so we've had to come up with some cool ways to adapt. See my long eyelashes?

INTERVIEWER: Yes.

CAMEL: Those keep the sand from blowing in my eyes. And believe it or not, my thick, shaggy coat actually keeps heat out. I bet I'm cooler than you are right now.

INTERVIEWER: I am really hot.

CAMEL: You better go and find some shade. Stay cool!

Survival Rules

In the desert, there are two rules for survival. First, keep cool. Second, get and keep water. Sounds easy, right? It's not. Remember, deserts can be hot, and they hardly ever get rain. Out in the desert, it really is adapt or die. Some animals have adapted in pretty interesting ways. Let's take a look at some of their amazing desert adaptations.

CHAPTER 3

COOL ADAPTATIONS

Getting out of the hot sun is the most obvious way to keep cool. But animals can't just run into their air-conditioned houses. They've had to find more creative ways to cool off. The Harris' antelope ground squirrel uses its tail. It arches its tail over its head like a built-in umbrella to get a little shade. But for many desert dwellers the answer isn't umbrella tails. They go underground.

Burrowing into the cool ground is common in the desert. The aardvark closes up its nostrils to keep the dirt out. Then it digs a tunnel into the ground to find some relief. The Gila monster has a lazy behavioral adaptation. This lizard is a burrow thief. A Gila monster will prowl around, looking for another animal's empty burrow. Before the owner returns, the Gila monster moves in.

Harris' antelope ground squirrel

burrow: to dig a hole

Gila monster

Sleepy Time

Do you ever get a little sleepy on a hot afternoon? Well, the spadefoot toad takes nap time to the extreme. Instead of working to find food and water, these toads sleep through the hottest parts of the year. This behavior is called **estivation**. During estivation, the toad's body slows way down. That way its body doesn't use much water or need more food. Other animals, like the round-tailed ground squirrel and desert tortoise, have this adaptation too.

estivation: sleeping during dry spells

spadefoot toad

Nighttime Fun

Once the sun goes down, the desert comes to life. Temperatures are much cooler at night and animals use that to their advantage. Many desert animals are **nocturnal**. They sleep all day and play all night. Soundlessly, long-nosed bats slip from their caves. They sip nectar from the night-blooming blossoms of cactus plants. Then they return to the caves before the blazing sun rises.

Potty Tricks

Here's a pretty gross adaptation. The turkey vulture keeps from overheating by peeing on itself. **Urohydrosis** is gross, but it works. These birds let the flow go. When the pee evaporates, it cools down the birds' bodies. Actually, it's not just watery pee. It's a mixture of pee and poop that splats all over the place.

urohydrosis: a big word for peeing down your legs

GROSS!

Peeing on their legs doesn't just keep vultures cool. Their urine has an acid in it that kills germs on their legs and feet.

GROSS!

When roadrunner chicks pee and poop, it all comes out in a little sac. When the sac pops out, the roadrunner's parents gobble it right up.

Open Wide

Roadrunners use their mouths to cool off. They open their beaks wide and move their throats in a fluttering motion. Gaping causes moisture in the roadrunner's mouth to evaporate. When the moisture turns from a liquid to a gas, it causes a cooling effect. It works a lot like sweating in humans.

bat-eared fox

Ear Conditioning

In the desert, ears aren't just for hearing. Having big ears is a huge plus. Animals like the bat-eared fox and the jackrabbit have adapted to have long, thin-skinned ears. Just below the skin are many blood vessels. When the animal sits in the shade, the blood in the vessels cools off fast. The bigger the ears, the quicker the blood gets cooled.

Desert Fishing

Okay, so this next animal hasn't figured out how to cool off, exactly. But its adaptation is still super cool. The amazing Devil's Hole pupfish lives in a water hole in Death Valley National Park. Not only does this fish (yes, a fish) live in the desert, it swims in water that can get as hot as 100 degrees Fahrenheit (38 degrees Celsius). Cool adaptation, indeed!

CHAPTER 4

WATERY ADAPTATIONS

Water is a necessity for life. Without it, an animal or plant would not be able to survive. Desert animals have had to adapt to an environment that doesn't provide much water. Their adaptations aren't pretty, but they work.

The kangaroo rat is a remarkable animal. These animals may never actually drink a drop of water their entire lives. They get all their water from the seeds they eat.

But here's the cool fact. The kangaroo rat's kidneys are five times more powerful than a human's. That means the rat's pee contains hardly any water. The less water that comes out, the more water that stays in the body to help the kangaroo rat survive.

Holding It In

The desert tortoise is like a living canteen. This tortoise can store a year's worth of water in its bladder. It doesn't have to worry about finding anything to drink for months. When it's needed, water is taken back into other parts of the tortoise's body.

If you come across a tortoise in the desert, don't pick it up! You'll frighten it so badly it will spray tortoise pee all over you. But it's not just bad for you. The tortoise could die if it can't find enough plants to replace the water you scared out of it.

Stuck in the Australian desert? You could stick the water-holding frog's rear end in your mouth and squeeze to squirt out some water.

The Australian water-holding frog holds water in its bladder too. When things get really dry, this frog burrows into the cool ground. It wraps itself in a cocoon of its own dry, dead skin. This frog can stay like that for seven years, because it doesn't use much water in that inactive state. When it finally rains again, the frog rips open its cocoon and has a tasty meal. It eats the dried out skin it has been hiding in.

Watery Roots

The naked mole rat spends almost all its life underground. It digs tunnels in search of roots and tubers. But this odd creature won't need a glass of water after all that work. It gets all the water it needs from the plants it finds underground.

Turkey Vulture Delight

If you're a turkey vulture, you'll love this roadkill recipe!

INGREDIENTS: 1 big, rotting piece of roadkill
Maggots, for extra protein

STEPS:

1. Wait for an animal to die. Don't worry, you'll smell its rotting flesh.

2. When you find some roadkill, stick your head deep inside the body. Rip out fat, greasy chunks. Swallow whole.

3. Keep eating until you have at least doubled your weight. This is a great way to get the water you need.

NOTE: The portions of this recipe are very large. You will be too heavy to fly after eating. If enemies approach, vomit huge, undigested portions on their faces. You'll be light enough to fly off. The enemy will forget about you in favor of the unexpected vomit treat.

ADAPTATION ADVENTURE

Today you're a desert research scientist. You've got a backpack full of water. Your hat is pulled down over your eyes. You've got a notebook stuffed with notes. And you've just discovered a brand new animal! You have to share your new discovery.

What adaptations does this animal have to survive? Where does it live? When is it active? How does it keep water? Draw a picture of this new animal. Write a paragraph describing its special adaptations and how it survives in the hot, dry desert.

The Western Banded gecko stores fat in its tail. This gecko can live off that tail fat for nine months.

Ferruginous pygmy owl

Surviving the Desert

It's not hard to see that extreme desert conditions call for every kind of crazy survival skill. From living in hot water to peeing on your legs to waking at night, adaptations make desert life possible. Desert life not only survives without much water, it thrives. Isn't that amazing?

TRUE LIVES OF SCIENTISTS

Scientists study the animals that live in the extreme desert environment. But it's not always easy. Many desert animals hide underground to stay cool.

Desert tortoises spend most of their time underground. Researchers have a hard time finding them. But the problem is that researchers *need* to find them. The desert tortoise is in danger of becoming extinct. And one part of protecting these animals is knowing how many there are left.

To the Dogs

Researchers realized that humans alone can't find all the desert tortoises. They wondered if dogs could sniff out tortoises above and below ground. To test their idea, researchers gathered some tortoises in a protected desert area. Then they trained dogs to sniff out tortoises. The dogs were trained to alert their handlers by sitting when they found something. A big part of the research was to see if the dogs would eat or harm the tortoises they found.

Did It Work?

Yes. The dogs found more desert tortoises than humans did. They even found babies that researchers almost always miss. And no tortoises were eaten! Dogs just might be able to help save this amazing desert creature.

GLOSSARY

ADAPT (uh-DAPT) — to change in order to survive; a change in an animal or plant is called an adaptation.

BURROW (BUHR-oh) — to dig a hole; a burrow can also be a hole in the ground that an animal makes.

CONTINENTAL (KAHN-tuh-nen-tuhl) — part of a continent; the continental United States is made up of the 48 states not including Hawaii or Alaska.

DNA (dee-en-AY) — the molecule that carries the genetic code that gives living things their special physical features

ESTIVATION (es-tuh-VAY-shun) — spending time in a deep sleep during dry or hot periods

NOCTURNAL (nok-TUR-nuhl) — active at night and resting during the day

SPECIES (SPEE-sheez) — a specific type of animal or plant

TUBER (TOO-bur) — the thick underground stem of a plant

UROHYDROSIS (YOOR-oh-hy-dro-sis) — urinating in order to cool the body

INTERNET SITES

FactHound offers a safe, fun way to find Internet sites related to this book. All of the sites on FactHound have been researched by our staff.

Here's how:

1. Visit *www.facthound.com*

2. Choose your grade level.

3. Type in this book ID **1429612665** for age-appropriate sites. You may also browse subjects by clicking on letters, or by clicking on pictures and words.

4. Click on the **Fetch It** button.

FactHound will fetch the best sites for you!

READ MORE

Bennett, Paul. *Desert Habitats*. Exploring Habitats. Milwaukee: Gareth Stevens, 2007.

Galko, Francine. *Desert Animals*. Animals in Their Habitats. Chicago: Heinemann, 2003.

Jackson, Kay. *Explore the Desert*. Explore the Biomes. Mankato, Minn.: Capstone Press, 2007.

INDEX